HEALING THROUGH WORDS

Other books by Rupi Kaur:

milk and honey

the sun and her flowers

home body

HEALING THROUGH WORDS

RUPI KAUR

Andrews McMeel
PUBLISHING®

Healing Through Words

Guided writing exercises designed by Rupi Kaur
to inspire creativity and healing

THIS BOOK BELONGS TO

rupikaur.com

POETRY

Poetry is the language of human emotion. It is air and fire and water and soil. Poetry is the breath in our lungs. The sighs. The stutters. Poetry is the first time you fall in love. And it breaks you. Poetry is hunger. The words hanging in the space between two mouths, right before the kiss. The thrill. Poetry is when your stomach is so heavy with butterflies, it drops down to your feet. Poetry is the light you walk away with after digging yourself out of grief. It is long conversations by the ocean. Poetry is winter's first snowfall. The smell of cookies in the oven. Poetry is sex. Elation. How we fight and make up. The journey. The story. Running and laughing. Laughing and running. Poetry is the might of one person, and the echo of billions. Our survival is poetry. Our lives are poetry. And the final act is writing it down.

WHO GETS TO BE CREATIVE?

Want to know what makes me sad? When someone tells me they're not creative.

How have we convinced millions of people that creativity is a skill only accessible to a select few, when the truth is that human beings are imaginative by nature; and it is our imaginations that have helped us survive hundreds of thousands of years. Our ability to come together, think, and solve problems is our collective creativity in motion.

When we were children, all of us were scribbling away, drawing and writing in our notebooks. At that tender age, we didn't see "creativity" as a skill; we saw it as something we did, along with another dozen things. This naivety and carelessness allowed us to create freely by taking risks. We played and explored for the sake of playing and exploring. We were present. We had fun.

But then, as we got older, we drew a little less. By middle school, our journals began to collect dust. In high school, most of us left writing and drawing behind altogether. How could we not? The weight of our responsibilities grew each year. We were so busy managing jam-packed school schedules and extracurricular activities, we didn't have the energy to do much else.

It's no wonder that as adults, our response to trying new things might be, "I can't. I'm not creative." This is often another way of saying, "I'm scared to try because I won't be any good, and if I'm not any good, I'll look like a fool." We started turning away from experiences that didn't make us look good on the first try.

Where's the freedom in that? Where's the discovery? We all have an inner child who wants to be heard, loved, and healed. We have to let them come out and play.

Creativity extends beyond the canvas and journal. Dancing is creative. Cleaning, writing an essay, coming up with an excuse for why you can't make it to Thanksgiving dinner this year is a creative act. So is organizing your closet, cooking, gardening, and browsing a library. We all get to be creative in whatever way we like.

WHO IS THIS BOOK FOR?

Healing Through Words is for anyone wanting to feel more connected to themselves. It is a collection of guided writing exercises designed to help you explore trauma, heartache, love, and healing in order to tap into your inner world. The exercises ask you to step into your vulnerability. You don't need to have any writing experience to complete them.

FREEWRITING

"I write because I don't know what I think until I read what I say."

—Flannery O'Connor

I took up writing during a difficult time in my life. I would set a timer, put my pen to paper, and write the first thing that came to mind. I would pour my heart out into my journal and it would bring my mind to ease. This form of freewriting helped me start my journey toward healing.

The exercises in this book are all freewriting exercises. Freewriting, often referred to as "stream of consciousness writing," is a form of deep listening where you let your thoughts flow out onto paper in real time. You're not worried about the quality of the writing. Your only goal is to write without inhibitions. As you're freewriting in this journal, don't erase or cross anything out. Don't overthink it. Just keep writing until it feels like you've said it all.

HOW I STARTED WRITING

My journey in poetry began back in high school when I started performing spoken word at local open mic nights.

Being onstage with a microphone felt absolutely magical. For the first time in my life I felt alive and worthy of being listened to. I'd write poems that were 4–5 minutes long and perform them in basements, community centers, and any venue that would have me.

I always say that it took me 21 years to write my first book, *milk and honey*. The first artistic project you birth is like that. It is a summation of all the years you lived before it. *milk and honey* wasn't something that I wrote—it was something that *happened* to me. A full sensory experience. To this day, writing it remains one of the most cathartic experiences of my life. Sometimes I close my eyes and think back to those years. Back to 2010. 2011. 2012. 2013. 2014. How vulnerable I was to receiving. To giving. To feeling. How cut open. How raw. How bleeding. How for the first time ever, I confronted the abuse my body had experienced. I stepped into my shoes with a confidence that scared the men around me. They didn't like how I openly talked about sexual abuse on the public stage. Regardless, I kept persuing this craft because it wasn't my job to help men remain comfortable. I was here for more. Luckily I had a group of powerful women around me who lifted me through the darkest times. Without them, I wouldn't be here. They gave me space to write, and a place to share it.

MY STYLE

I like to think that I write two types of poetry. The first is **performance poetry**, which is poetry that comes to life on the stage. It is usually longer and written to be performed. Performance poetry weaves a story and pulls the listener into a new universe. For me, writing performance poetry is like writing music. And performing it onstage is playing that music live.

Every poem comes out of me in beats and syllables, with its own unique melody and rhythm. I think this may be because I grew up listening to Punjabi poetry, and within Punjabi culture, poetry is an oral tradition. One of my favorite memories growing up was watching the women in my community gather in circles to do *giddha* (a popular folk dance for women in the Punjab region). While doing *giddha*, they sang *boliyan* (couplet style verses). Getting together to do *giddha* was one of the few times women had the opportunity to gather with other women, without any men around. They would let their hair down, dance, laugh, and be joyous. They would take turns freestyling some of the funniest verses I've ever heard, taking jabs at their overbearing mother-in-laws, talking shit about the neighbors, their siblings, and each other. They'd sing *boliyan* full of sexual jokes that would leave you on the floor laughing. In this safe space, everything and everyone was fair game. This is where women would blow off steam before heading back to what were often difficult lives.

So you see, poetry for me has always been written to be performed. It's about healing and being accessible to community.

The second type of poetry I write is what I refer to as **paper poetry**, which is poetry that is most alive on paper. I believe that paper poetry has the strongest impact when read to oneself. How the poem looks visually on the page plays a big role in how the reader will feel it. Every element is intentional. The punctuation used or not used is meant to give the poem a certain rhythm. The line breaks are deliberate. I like to break at places where the melody is supposed to hang. I may end a line where I want to emphasize a certain word.

Although paper poetry can come in various lengths and styles, I like to experiment with more succinct and shorter pieces. I try to use words that are going to drop into the reader's heart like gravity.

When you're in the middle of having your heart broken, or experiencing something traumatic, reality doesn't reveal itself slowly, it pierces you like a bullet, fast and hard. I want my paper poetry to do the same, which is why it's direct. My intention is for it to hit hard and fast, like that metaphorical bullet. Every word I use plays an important role. During the editing process, if a word can be removed because it doesn't serve a purpose, I remove it. I don't want any extra words hanging around.

I share this with you to give you insight into how I write and why. You don't need to write in the same way. You need to write whichever way makes you feel alive and seen. In this book, we will be experimenting with both shorter and longer pieces.

TIPS (BEFORE YOU GET STARTED)

1) All the exercises in this book are freewriting exercises. This means you're going to do your best to write the first thought that comes to you—don't edit, erase, or censor yourself. It doesn't matter if what you write makes sense or not. All that matters is that you give up control and let your subconscious take the wheel.

2) The exercises are divided into chapters. Ideally, you would complete the book from beginning to end. By no means do you have to do that. Feel free to go through the exercises however feels right for you.

3) For many of the exercises, I provide prompts that are meant to spark creativity. A prompt might be a question I ask you to answer, or a word or phrase that acts as the beginning of your piece.

4) For some exercises, I ask you to close your eyes and do some deep breathing before you start writing. Don't skip the breath work. Do it! It will help you relax, which in turn will spark creativity.

5) You don't need to be a writer or poet to get the full experience of these exercises. You just need to write—that's all.

6) To make directions clear, I will refer to what you're writing as "poems" or "pieces." These are just instructional labels and they can mean whatever you want.

7) Poetry is so much more than what you were taught in high school. I promise you that everyone can write a poem. Your poems don't need to rhyme or be a collection of stanzas. When I ask you to write a poem, it means to be vulnerable and express raw emotions. In this journal, that can result in ten words or a hundred. It can mean you are writing in stanzas or paragraphs. It can mean you're rhyming or not rhyming. The only rule to writing a poem in this journal is allowing yourself to write freely.

8) If a certain exercise triggers you, skip it. It's not worth doing. You can always return to it at a later time.

9) For some exercises, I suggest that you set a timer. The timer is meant to guide and support you through the experience. However, don't feel constrained by it. It's alright if you go over or under time.

10) If you need more space to complete the exercises, feel free to complete them in your personal journal.

11) Chapter one, "hurting," is about trauma. It is the most emotionally taxing of the four chapters. Take breaks as you work through it. You may find that even a 15-minute exercise exhausts you. That's perfectly normal. Talking about trauma takes a lot of energy out of us, so don't be hard on yourself. Go at a pace that feels safe and healthy.

12) These exercises shouldn't feel like work—they should feel like an exhale. Let go, and let the words flow.

if i knew what
safety looked like
i would have spent
less time falling into
arms that were not

milk and honey, page 21

CHAPTER ONE

HURTING

It was the experience of sexual and physical abuse that initially drew me to write. This particular violence went so deep, it silenced me. I felt voiceless and unable to tell anyone about what I referred to as the "bad stuff."

Then, around the time I was 18-years-old, I went to see this new therapist at school. In our first session, he introduced me to the word "trauma." The word struck me like a knife. *Trauma*. That's how the therapist referred to my "bad stuff." I remember sitting on his stiff leather couch in silence, unsure of what to say because normal people like me didn't experience trauma. "Trauma" sounded like a word used to describe life-threatening car accidents, or the horrors soldiers experienced during war.

In our second session, the therapist said I may be experiencing PTSD (post-traumatic stress disorder). I remember trying really hard not to roll my eyes. At the end of the session, I walked out and never saw him again.

Years later, I realized the therapist wasn't being dramatic. Sexual, domestic, mental, physical, and emotional abuse *is* trauma, and survivors of this trauma fall under the umbrella of those who can experience PTSD. I guess when you experience something so traumatic at a young age, and so often, it becomes normalized. As a child, your frame of reference for what's "normal" becomes skewed. With this new information, I accepted that I needed to take steps toward healing.

Writing became a part of that healing journey quite quickly. It was difficult to openly talk about what I'd survived, so I turned to my journal because writing felt safe. As I began to find the words for what happened, I began to feel free. This is how the seeds of my first book, *milk and honey*, were planted.

The exercises in this chapter explore different themes surrounding trauma. Go through them at your own pace. Your safety and well-being come first. If you feel that you don't have any trauma to explore, that's okay. You don't have to have trauma to dive deep. You are already rich and never-ending. Trauma isn't what defines us. It isn't what makes us interesting. Our *voice* and how we *use* it is. If there are exercises that ask you to reflect on a certain experience, and you haven't had that experience, just refer to something else. No matter the degree, we all have painful experiences, and all of them are worth investigating. Let your inner artist come out and play. If you need to tweak the exercises to make them work for you, please feel free to do so. I hope that what you write in this chapter shows you how much of a warrior you are.

EXERCISE 1	WHAT TRAUMA LOOKS LIKE

1) Close your eyes and take 10 deep breaths, nice and slowly.

After the tenth breath, spend some moments meditating on the word "trauma."

Then, draw what trauma looks like in the space below. When your eyes were closed and you were meditating on the word, what did you see?

2) Observe your drawing and jot down a few words or simple phrases that come to mind when you look at it:

3) Randomly select 4 of the words or phrases you jotted dotted down above, and list them here:

1.

2.

3.

4.

You will now freewrite 4 paragraphs or stanzas using the 4 words/phrases you selected above, in chronological order. Each paragraph/stanza must include a word/phrase from the above list, in their numbered order.

GUIDELINES

🕐 **Set a timer for 10 minutes.** Keep an eye on the timer, and spend 2–3 minutes writing each paragraph or stanza. If you go over or under time, that's okay. The timer is there to support you.

» Your first paragraph must include the first word/phrase you selected.

» Your second paragraph must include the second word/phrase selected.

» Your third paragraph must include the third word/phrase selected.

» Your fourth paragraph must include the fourth word/phrase selected.

» By the end of the exercise, all 4 words/phrases will have been used in your piece.

» There is no need to use the word/phrase more than once.

» Remember, this is a freewriting exercise, so whether what you write makes sense or not, go wherever your thoughts take you.

» Your piece begins with the prompt "*The crack in the.*" These opening words are meant to spark creativity. Complete this phrase and continue writing.

🕐 **Start your timer and begin freewriting:**

The crack in the

EXERCISE 2	WHAT YOU KEEP HIDDEN

🕐 **Set a timer for 10 minutes.** Read the prompt, and freewrite your thoughts:

The thing I am most scared of people finding out about me is

EXERCISE 3	LETTER WRITING

An exercise I do often, especially when I feel writer's block, is letter writing. By leaning into something as personal and familiar as writing a letter, this exercise takes the pressure off of having to figure out what I'm going to write about on a day I feel stuck. Instead, my creative attention is directed toward what I already know, which is comforting.

I also write to specific emotions I've been experiencing. For example, I've written many letters to "fear." Doing so has helped me have a conversation and confront fear, rather than try to bury it.

I usually spend anywhere from 15–30 minutes writing these letters.

Below is a list of 7 letter writing prompts. For this exercise, select one, and write your letter in the space provided. (Although there's only space to complete one of the letters in this journal, feel free to complete the others in your personal journal at a later time. I also love to repeat prompts I've used in the past. It helps to look back and compare results to see what's changed or stayed the same.)

Set a timer for 15 minutes. Then, select one of the following prompts and begin freewriting:

» Write a letter to the person whose touch hurt you

» Write a letter to your father, from the perspective of your 7-year-old self

» Write a letter to your 9-year-old self, from the perspective of your 80-year-old self

» Write a letter to a traumatic memory or moment

» Write a letter to "self-doubt"

» Write a letter to the parts of you that are still hurting

» Write a letter to your mom when she was pregnant with you, from the perspective of your unborn self

EXERCISE 4	WHAT AM I?

Take some time to examine the following drawing:

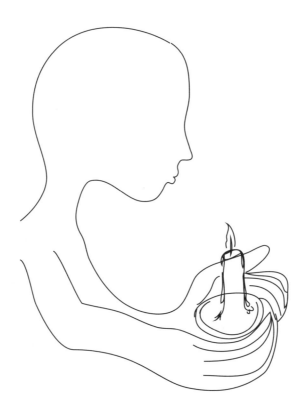

Now, write down what this drawing brings up for you. What was the first thing that you thought of when you observed it? Does the drawing have a story? What is it trying to communicate?

🕐 **Set a timer for 10 minutes and begin:**

EXERCISE 5	PEACH PITS

I love how a few words strung together have the power to tell a story. Sikh poetry is where I first noticed this.

I grew up doing *kirtan*: the musical art of singing Sikh *shabads* (hymns) and playing the harmonium alongside them. In junior high, I used to go home after *kirtan* class, and sit with one of my parents to study the latest *shabad* assigned to me. We'd spend hours discussing a single line—that's how much depth just a few words had. This is how I fell in love with trying to say more with less.

In high school, I read this famous "6-word story" for the first time, and my fascination with short, concise prose grew even stronger. The poem, possibly written by Ernest Hemingway, read:

For sale: baby shoes, never worn.

Oufffff!!!! This line punched me in the gut and left me speechless. What a heartbreaking story, told in just 6 words!!!! This was the moment I began to see writing poetry as a sort of puzzle making. I asked myself, how can I construct the story I want without wasting any puzzle pieces? Meaning, how could I make my point without wasting words?

For someone who grew up struggling to express herself, words were sacred. Because of physical and sexual abuse, I grew up feeling invisible and voiceless, so when I started performing and writing poetry, I wanted my words to puncture through the noise so they couldn't be missed. I refused to be invisible any longer. I refused to hold on to my trauma as if I were responsible for it. I refused to carry the guilt and shame, when it wasn't mine to carry.

My writing style reflects this. It was a stylistic choice to write succintly, without the bells and whistles. In healing, communication was key, so I removed any extra padding in my writing. I needed to present the *exact* words to my audience, without distractions.

I like to describe my shorter poems (the ones that are 1–4 lines), as *peach pits*.

A lot of people look at the size of these shorter pieces and assume they don't take very long to write. This couldn't be further from the truth. Each of these peach pit poems start off much longer, some a page or two long.

During the editing process, I cut out lines I don't like, which usually reduces the size of my draft by 25 percent. Then I determine the "thesis" of my poem. I like for a poem to have a single thesis, so that my message is delivered clearly.

Once I establish the thesis of the poem, I cut out any lines that don't support it. Then I cut out any words hanging around not doing anything.

This process is like removing the skin of the peach, then slowly digging through the fruity meat, until finally, I hit the center—the peach pit. I take this peach pit, and present it to my reader on a silver platter. I love giving them the core essence of what I am trying to say so that it is felt immediately.

Of course, not all my writing fits into this style. Some poems, especially my spoken word poems, are so long they take a whole 5 minutes to recite. There's a time and place for each style. The trick, I guess, is picking which style to deliver which message. I use the peach pit style when I want the poem to hit hard and fast, like a metaphorical bullet.

Here are some of my poems that illustrate the "peach pit" concept:

> *i've had sex* she said
> but i don't know
> what making love
> feels like
>
> *milk and honey,* page 20

if i knew what
safety looked like
i would have spent
less time falling into
arms that were not

milk and honey, page 21

he was supposed to be
the first male love of your life
you still search for him
everywhere

- father

milk and honey, page 16

In this 2-part exercise, you will be writing your own peach pit poems. We will go through the entire process together. Remember, don't overthink it, and have fun.

1) For the first part of this exercise, write a lengthy piece about a time that you felt ignored.

🕐 **Set a timer for 5 minutes and begin:**

2) For the second part of this exercise, you will be editing your piece into a peach pit poem, and I will take you through the process step-by-step.

» First, go back to part 1 and read your piece from beginning to end. After you're done, define the thesis of your piece in one sentence and write it in the space below. Remember, the thesis of your piece is the core message (if you're having trouble deciding on the thesis, write down what you would tell me if I asked you to summarize your poem in one line):

» Now that you've established a thesis, reread your piece, and cross out any lines that don't support or that distract from your thesis. Once you've established the lines you're going to keep, write them in the space below:

» Using a scrap piece of paper or your personal journal, edit what you just wrote until it's condensed into 4 lines. It will take many pages and rewrites to complete this part. As you're editing, don't forget your thesis! The goal in this part is to slowly, but eventually, settle on 4 lines that support your thesis in the best possible way ("best" is subjective here).

As you are editing, make as many changes as you like. You can even add new lines if you think they're stronger.

Sometimes, by the end of the editing process, I've rewritten the poem 50–100 times. This process can take hours, weeks, or months. Sometimes I never finish the process and the poem remains unfinished. For the purposes of this exercise, we won't be taking hours or weeks. Instead, keep editing your poem until you land on 4 lines you love. Write those 4 lines below:

» Now, revisit the 4 lines on the previous page. Try to make them shorter by removing unnecessary words or shortening phrases. The purpose of this part is to get your 4 lines to be as potent as possible, while still supporting your thesis in the strongest way you can.

For inspiration, revisit the peach pit poems I provided as examples on pages 20–21. Once you've settled on what you consider the most potent version, write your peach pit poem below:

EXERCISE 6	VISITING MY YOUNGER SELF

For this exercise, we'll be drawing inspiration from my love of performance poetry.

As I mentioned in the introduction, my journey in poetry began on the stage, back in high school, when I started performing spoken word poetry at local community centers and open mic nights. Performance poetry is poetry that comes to life on the stage. These poems are written to be read aloud. My spoken word poems range anywhere from 2–6 minutes long. Yours can be anywhere in that timeframe.

For this exercise, feel free to write about any topic. You may end up with one really long paragraph that goes on for pages, or you may end up with smaller paragraphs. The style doesn't matter. What matters is the content. Weave a story for us. Use imagery and metaphors. Get descriptive and emotional.

The only rule is that your piece must include all of the following words, using the instructions provided in the guidelines:

- » Laugh
- » Lion
- » Fork
- » Blue
- » Hundred
- » Water
- » Butterfly
- » Cloud
- » Gem
- » Clock

GUIDELINES

» You have two options for how to use all the words on the list. Pick one:

Option one: Begin writing with the intention to use the first word (laugh) early on in the piece. Then, when you feel your thoughts slowing down and you're wondering what to write next, randomly select one of the words on the list, let it inspire a new thought, insert it into the piece, and keep writing (don't forget to cross out the word after you use it). Repeat this until all the words on the list have been used.

Option two: Let the timer lead you. Hit start, begin writing, and every 2 minutes, pick a word from the list and include it in your piece right then and there. Continue until all the words have been used.

» Begin by closing your eyes and taking a few minutes to yourself in silence. Breathe in. Breathe out. Center yourself in your body. Once you feel grounded, open your eyes.

» I've already started your piece off with a prompt.

🕐 **Set a timer for 20 minutes and begin freewriting:**

If I could visit my younger self I would go back to the day when

EXERCISE 7	MOTHER

We often hide our pain from those closest to us. Sharing our pain with them would feel like a giant burden being lifted from our shoulders, but it's hard to open up.

For this exercise, write a poem to your mother, confessing any hurt you may be experiencing or have experienced in the past. It doesn't have to be hurt that she's caused—it can be any hurt that you've felt throughout life. Read the prompt I've provided and start freewriting:

Dear Mother
One thing I need you to know is

EXERCISE 8	FEAR

1) Make a list of up to 15 things you are afraid of:

»

»

»

»

»

»

»

»

»

»

»

»

»

»

»

2) From the above list, randomly select 5 fears. Starting on the next page, elaborate on each fear by exploring why and where it comes from, what it connects to, and how it affects your life:

Fear One: _____

(Why and where does this fear come from? What's it connected to?
How does it affect my life?)

Fear Two: _____

(Why and where does this fear come from? What's it connected to?
How does it affect my life?)

Fear Three: _____

(Why and where does this fear come from? What's it connected to?
How does it affect my life?)

Fear Four: _____

(Why and where does this fear come from? What's it connected to?
How does it affect my life?)

Fear Five: _____
(Why and where does this fear come from? What's it connected to?
How does it affect my life?)

3) Having fears doesn't make us weak—it makes us human. Our brains are hardwired to feel fear in order to help us survive. Although the human brain is a magnificent thing, sometimes it can't tell the difference between a rational or irrational fear.

An example of a rational fear is worrying that you won't be able to pay next month's rent because you got laid off and have no savings. This fear is rational because you have facts that prove how the fear could become a reality.

An example of an irrational fear is worrying your coworkers are going to hate the presentation you have to give on Friday. This fear is irrational because you've spent weeks practicing your presentation and know the information really well. In fact, you've never tanked on a presentation before, so you have no reason to believe that you'll tank now.

This fear is irrational because it's not rooted in fact—it's only rooted in feeling. Now, just because it's rooted in feeling doesn't mean the fear isn't real. It just means that according to the facts, there is a higher chance your presentation will go well, rather than go poorly.

Studying our irrational fears can tell us a lot about our psyche. A lot of these irrational fears are planted in our brains at a young age, perhaps by our environment and the people who raised us.

Maybe we fear no one will love us because when we were 5-years-old our parents left us home alone with a really mean babysitter while they worked overtime.

Maybe we fear no one will date us because our first crush called us "unattractive."

Ignoring irrational fears only gives them more power. I've found that the best way to free myself from irrational fears is by talking to them directly. After understanding the fear, I like to make a list of outcomes from best to worst that could occur if this fear were to become a reality. I then review the list and select which outcome is most likely to occur. Usually what happens at this stage of the exercise is that my irrational fear is eased because the outcome that's most realistic is not as scary as the one I was afraid of.

Now I'd like you to revisit the 5 fears you wrote about in part 2, and answer the following questions:

Fear One: _____

What's the worst possible outcome that can happen?

What's the best possible outcome that can happen?

What are 2–3 other possible outcomes in between?

On a scale of 1–10, how likely is it for the worst possible outcome to occur?

1.	2.	3.	4.	5.	6.	7.	8.	9.	10.
Least likely									Most likely

Based on the above likelihood, how rational or irrational is your fear?

1.	2.	3.	4.	5.	6.	7.	8.	9.	10.
Completely rational									Completely irrational

Now, talk to the fear directly.

» If the fear is irrational and highly unlikely to happen, have a conversation with it and share why it's time for it to leave. Fear isn't your enemy. Fear is just trying to warn and protect you. It's your job to investigate what worries it has. Finally, thank the fear for alerting you, and explain why you'll be safe.

» If the fear is rational and highly likely to happen, write about how you will make space for it, how you'd like to work together, and why you'll be okay.

Fear Two: _____

What's the worst possible outcome that can happen?

What's the best possible outcome that can happen?

What are 2–3 other possible outcomes in between?

On a scale of 1–10, how likely is it for the worst possible outcome to occur?

1.	2.	3.	4.	5.	6.	7.	8.	9.	10.
Least likely									Most likely

Based on the above likelihood, how rational or irrational is your fear?

1.	2.	3.	4.	5.	6.	7.	8.	9.	10.
Completely rational									Completely irrational

Now, talk to the fear directly.

» If the fear is irrational and highly unlikely to happen, have a conversation with it and share why it's time for it to leave. Fear isn't your enemy. Fear is just trying to warn and protect you. It's your job to investigate what worries it has. Finally, thank the fear for alerting you, and explain why you'll be safe.

» If the fear is rational and highly likely to happen, write about how you will make space for it, how you'd like to work together, and why you'll be okay.

Fear Three: _____

What's the worst possible outcome that can happen?

What's the best possible outcome that can happen?

What are 2–3 other possible outcomes in between?

On a scale of 1–10, how likely is it for the worst possible outcome to occur?

1.	2.	3.	4.	5.	6.	7.	8.	9.	10.
Least likely									Most likely

Based on the above likelihood, how rational or irrational is your fear?

1.	2.	3.	4.	5.	6.	7.	8.	9.	10.
Completely rational									Completely irrational

Now, talk to the fear directly.

» If the fear is irrational and highly unlikely to happen, have a conversation with it and share why it's time for it to leave. Fear isn't your enemy. Fear is just trying to warn and protect you. It's your job to investigate what worries it has. Finally, thank the fear for alerting you, and explain why you'll be safe.

» If the fear is rational and highly likely to happen, write about how you will make space for it, how you'd like to work together, and why you'll be okay.

Fear Four: _____

What's the worst possible outcome that can happen?

What's the best possible outcome that can happen?

What are 2–3 other possible outcomes in between?

On a scale of 1–10, how likely is it for the worst possible outcome to occur?

1.	2.	3.	4.	5.	6.	7.	8.	9.	10.
Least likely									Most likely

Based on the above likelihood, how rational or irrational is your fear?

1.	2.	3.	4.	5.	6.	7.	8.	9.	10.
Completely rational									Completely irrational

Now, talk to the fear directly.

» If the fear is irrational and highly unlikely to happen, have a conversation with it and share why it's time for it to leave. Fear isn't your enemy. Fear is just trying to warn and protect you. It's your job to investigate what worries it has. Finally, thank the fear for alerting you, and explain why you'll be safe.

» If the fear is rational and highly likely to happen, write about how you will make space for it, how you'd like to work together, and why you'll be okay.

Fear Five: _____

What's the worst possible outcome that can happen?

What's the best possible outcome that can happen?

What are 2–3 other possible outcomes in between?

On a scale of 1–10, how likely is it for the worst possible outcome to occur?

1.	2.	3.	4.	5.	6.	7.	8.	9.	10.
Least likely									Most likely

Based on the above likelihood, how rational or irrational is your fear?

1.	2.	3.	4.	5.	6.	7.	8.	9.	10.
Completely rational									Completely irrational

Now, talk to the fear directly.

» If the fear is irrational and highly unlikely to happen, have a conversation with it and share why it's time for it to leave. Fear isn't your enemy. Fear is just trying to warn and protect you. It's your job to investigate what worries it has. Finally, thank the fear for alerting you, and explain why you'll be safe.

» If the fear is rational and highly likely to happen, write about how you will make space for it, how you'd like to work together, and why you'll be okay.

EXERCISE 9	WORD ASSOCIATION

Think fast:

1) What's the first word that comes to mind when you hear the word "**silence**"?

2) What's the first word that comes to mind when you hear the word "**remember**"?

3) What's the first word that comes to mind when you hear the word "**imperfect**"?

4) What's the first word that comes to mind when you hear the word "**apocalypse**"?

Now take the 4 bolded words above (**silence, remember, imperfect, apocalypse**), along with the 4 words you wrote down and write 4 paragraphs/stanzas about an experience that made you angry.

The first paragraph must include the word pairing in question 1:
silence & _____
(The word you wrote in association with "silence")

The second paragraph must include the word pairing in question 2:
remember & _____
(The word you wrote in association with "remember")

The third paragraph must include the word pairing in question 3:

imperfect & _____

(The word you wrote in association with "imperfect")

The fourth paragraph must include the word pairing in question 4:

apocalypse & _____

(The word you wrote in association with "apocalypse")

🕐 **Spend 5–7 minutes writing each paragraph.**

EXERCISE 10	ANXIETY

If you are alive and human, you've experienced anxiety at some point in your life. I always joke that anxious people are the normal ones, because who in their right mind could live in this world and not be anxious?! Seriously, nonanxious people: how? Please advise.

When I was younger, I didn't know that my chest pain, breathing issues, and stomachaches were symptoms of anxiety. I didn't have the language to describe what was happening then. However, over time, I started noticing how different parts of my body reacted to anxiety. My hands would tremble. Anxiety made me feel lightheaded, weak, and exhausted. Sometimes it felt like someone was standing on my chest while wearing heavy boots. I'd be left gasping for air.

Becoming aware of these symptoms and how they affected me allowed me to be more compassionate toward myself. For this exercise, you will be tapping into different areas and functions of your body to see what they reveal about your anxiety. The only rule is that you must answer each question with *exactly* 3 sentences. No more, no less.

I know I've been telling you to freewrite the first thoughts that come to you, but complete this exercise a lot slower than previous ones. Be intentional with your 3-sentence answer (you'll see why later).

1) When you start to get anxious, which part of your body does anxiety manifest in first?

2) In what other areas of the body is the anxiety felt?

3) What does anxiety feel like in your throat?

4) Are there situations where you hold your breath unnecessarily, without being aware of it? (For example, sometimes I unknowingly hold my breath as I type, drive, and take pictures. Also, when I'm around people who intimidate, or make me feel unsafe.)

5) Which part of your body feels most exhausted after being anxious?

6) What does anxiety feel like in your stomach?

7) What soothes your body when it is anxious?

8) You just wrote a total of 21 sentences (through questions 1–7). You will now use these to construct 3 poems that are each 7 lines long. Don't use more than 2 lines from the same question. Use every line once, and only once. If you'd like, you can make minor changes to the sentences to help with flow, grammar, or tense. Use a pencil for this exercise, as you may need to erase and make changes.

This part of the exercise is more about editing than writing. The goal is to see if you can take something you've already written and imagine it in a whole new way. Sometimes there are hidden gems in front of us that we only discover once we shake things up. Sometimes, when I feel uninspired, I revisit old writing to see if it can be adapted in a new way. By the end of this exercise you may discover something you love. At the very least, it'll be an interesting experiment.

Poem 1:

Poem 2:

Poem 3:

EXERCISE 11	A LIST POEM

A list poem is a poem written in the format of a list. It's an inventory of people, places, things, or thoughts. The list can be written however you'd like: jot notes, long lines, bullet points, or numbered. A well-written list poem tells a story through the items it lists.

Here's a list poem I wrote about depression:

depression is:
- silent
- i never hear it coming
- sits at the corner of my bed
  waits for me to get up
  walks into me like a ghost
  and refuses to leave my body
- depression is the amusement park after everyone's left
- a ghost town that i'm lost in
- an empty road at 2 a.m.
- empty pizza boxes
- missed calls from friends
- an abandoned shopping mall
- the desire to forget where i am
- a weight tied to my throat
  hanging down to my belly
- feeling somewhere between living and dead
- it feels like i'm undying

For this exercise, I want you to create your own list poem based on any of the following topics:

» Grief

» Anxiety

» Failure

» Shame

» Pain

» Self-doubt

» Hope

» Losing

» Trying

» Friendship

GUIDELINES

🕐 **Set a timer for 10–15 minutes.**

» Your list poem can be as long as you'd like.

» Turn the page and start freewriting.

_____ is:
(Write your selected topic here.)

| EXERCISE 12 | TO THE PEOPLE WHO'VE TOUCHED MY BODY |

Write a letter addressed to all the people who've touched your body.

🕐 **Set a timer for 15 minutes and begin freewriting:**

To all the people who've touched my body,

| EXERCISE 13 | BEDROOM WALLS |

Read the prompt, and freewrite your thoughts:

If the walls of my bedroom could talk they'd say

love will come
and when love comes
love will hold you
love will call your name
and you will melt
sometimes though
love will hurt you but
love will never mean to
love will play no games
cause love knows life
has been hard enough already

milk and honey, page 60

CHAPTER TWO
LOVING

I first started writing poetry because I wanted to explore what it meant to be a woman. We live in a patriarchal world where gender-based violence is widespread. Through poetry, I wanted to tap into stories surrounding this violence in order to write words that gave me hope.

I wrote about this violence for years, until a voice inside me said, "I'm tired. You write about how terrible the violence is, but you do realize that no one can take away your power, right?!"

It was this defiant voice that gave me permission to start exploring lighter themes and not be knee-deep in trauma all the time. I then began writing about love and sexuality. This helped me redefine toxic ideas of love and replace them with sustainable ones. I wrote about pleasure, orgasms, sex, and masturbation as a way to reclaim my body. By doing this, I realized I am allowed to take the time to heal from sexual trauma, while simultaneously enjoying the pleasures my body is capable of feeling. I am not just what happened to me. I am multifaceted. As a survivor, exploring these topics is essential.

Through the exercises in this chapter, I hope you are able to take a closer look at what love means to you, what you want it to mean in the years to come, and what you are deserving of.

EXERCISE 1	LOVE

In the space below, write down every word you can think of when you hear the word "love":

🕐 **1) Set a timer for 1 minute and begin.** As soon as the timer ends, move on to part 2:

2) Now describe "love" without using the word "love," and any of the other words you listed in part 1.

🕐 **Set a timer for 15 minutes and begin:**

EXERCISE 2	LOVE IS NOT

Write a list of what you think love is not.

(If you need to jog your memory about what a list poem is, refer to page 62.)

Set a timer for 10 minutes and begin:

Love is not:

EXERCISE 3	WHAT AM I?

Take some time to examine the following drawing:

Now, write down what this drawing brings up for you. What was the first thing that you thought of when you observed it? Does the drawing have a story? What is it trying to communicate?

🕐 **Set a timer for 10 minutes and begin:**

EXERCISE 4	DECLARATION, NEEDS, GOAL

i do not want to have you

to fill the empty parts of me

i want to be full on my own

i want to be so complete

i could light a whole city

and then

i want to have you

cause the two of us combined

could set it on fire

milk and honey, page 59

I wrote this poem during a time I was learning to redefine love.

I used to allow people to hurt me because I thought it was the price I had to pay for the rare moments they made me feel good. Luckily, I learned that I deserved better and could no longer excuse toxic behavior. In fact, I didn't need someone else to make me feel good, because I had the power to do that for myself.

The question I was trying to answer while writing this poem was: What do I deserve?

I wrote about how I deserved someone who invested in the relationship just as much as I did. Someone who was not intimidated by my voice. If I was going to make space for another human being in my life, I wanted them to have qualities that would amplify my light, not dim it.

For this exercise, let's break this poem down and study it in parts.

The poem starts off with a **declaration**:

> i do not want to have you
> to fill the empty parts of me

It follows with a statement of **needs**:

> i want to be full on my own
> i want to be so complete
> i could light a whole city

It concludes with an intended **goal**:

> and then
> i want to have you
> cause the two of us combined
> could set it on fire

This declaration-needs-goal format helps me find answers when I'm going through a period of transition. This format also has the ability to tell a succinct story. The declaration, need, and goal function like a beginning, middle, and end.

For this exercise, you'll be writing a poem with a declaration, need, and goal statement. I've given you a prompt at the start of each section; all you have to do is fill in the rest.

GUIDELINES

» **Declaration:** Make any declaration of your choice. This section will reveal an area of focus and set the tone for the rest of the poem.

» **Needs:** What is it that you need, that you aren't receiving?

» **Goal:** How do you want the future to be different? What are you hoping for? What do you expect? What will you accept? What will you reject?

1)

Start your poem off with a **declaration**:

I will not _____

_____

_____

_____

Follow with a statement of **needs**:

I am too _____

_____

_____

_____

Conclude with an intended **goal**:

The one who deserves me will _____

_____

_____

_____

2) Now let's try another:

Start your poem off with a **declaration**:

What you did was _____

_____

_____

_____

Follow with a statement of **needs**:

Imagine _____

_____

_____

_____

Conclude with an intended **goal**:

Unless you are _____

_____

_____

_____

3) And another:

Start your poem off with a **declaration**:

I don't care _____

_____

_____

_____

Follow with a statement of **needs**:

I want _____

_____

_____

_____

Conclude with an intended **goal**:

and _____

_____

_____

_____

4) And finally, write one completely on your own:

Start your poem off with a **declaration**:

_____

_____

_____

_____

Follow with a statement of **needs**:

_____

_____

_____

_____

Conclude with an intended **goal**:

_____

_____

_____

_____

EXERCISE 5	PASSION

🕐 **1) Set a timer for 10 minutes.** In the space below, draw what "passion" looks like.

2) For the second part of this exercise, you will be writing a sonnet about passion (based on your drawing in part 1). A sonnet is a 14-line poem. There are many ways to write sonnets, but since we aren't too concerned with technique or style at this stage, don't worry about that. All you need to do is write 14 lines.

I've given you prompts for each line. Use your drawing to help you fill in the blanks:

Passion looks like a _____

At first sight _____

_____

It wants to _____

Sounds like a _____

Reminds me why I _____

when it touches me _____

_____

I've never seen _____

Helplessly _____

_____

The last time _____

Imagine _____

Finally _____

EXERCISE 6	PLEASURE

Answer the following:

If you've ever felt shame telling the person you're sleeping with about what you want in bed, what would you ask for if that shame didn't exist?

EXERCISE 7	LIGHTS ON

Make a list of the following:

1) What turns you on?

2) Based on your list above, write a poem about experiencing some (or all) of those turn-ons.

    As a woman, my pleasure is not always prioritized, which is why I find it empowering to write sex-positive poems. They've helped cement the fact that my body is not just for pleasuring others. I deserve pleasure too.

Here's an example of a sex-positive poem I wrote in *home body*:

my body is so hot from wanting you

i'm spilling by the time we take our clothes off

i want the kind of love that

transcends me

into another realm

i want you so deep

we enter the spirit world

go from being gentle to rough

i want eye contact

spread my legs to

opposite ends of the room

and look with your fingers

i want my soul to be touched

by the tip of yours

i want to come

out of this room

different people

- can you do that

home body, page 81

Now it's your turn. **Set a timer for 15 minutes**. I've provided a prompt to help you get started:

You pin my hands

EXERCISE 8	A PROSE STORY

1) Answer the following:

    a. What is your favorite place in your hometown? _____

    b. What's the last thing you ate? _____

    c. What's your favorite piece of clothing? _____

    d. Circle one of the following:

      Mysterious   Arrogant   Boring

    e. Circle one of the following:

      Do   Do not

2) Take the answers from above and fill them into their appropriate blanks:

This date is taking place at _____ .
                    (Your answer from part a)

The two of you are eating _____ .
                 (Your answer from part b)

You're wearing _____ .
          (Your answer from part c)

Halfway through the date you notice this person is really _____ .
                              (Your answer from part d)

In the end, the two of you _____ hook up.

(Your answer from part e)

3) Now we get to the writing. Picture this: it's Friday night and you're on a first date. All those blank spaces you filled in step 2 outline the details of your date. Given those details, write about what would occur on this date. Make sure to include all 5 underlined details.

GUIDELINES

🕐 **Set a timer for 20 minutes.**

» There are many ways you can write about this date. One way is to write about the date as if it's happening in the present moment. Another way is to write about it in the past tense, as if you're telling your best friends about it the following morning. Pick one, be creative, and have fun!

EXERCISE 9	MAKE A TOAST

Whether it's at a birthday party or anniversary, I love a good speech!!! My favorite kind of speech is one that's given in the spur of the moment.

Let's say I'm at a friend's birthday party and having a really good time. I'm that person who loves to make everyone go around in a circle and say nice things about the birthday girl. Those moments when people are improvising allow them to be more vulnerable. They say things that are emotional, sweet, funny, even corny. Their words invite a burst of awwwwws and ouuuuus from the crowd. Those are the speeches I love.

An unplanned speech is much like freewriting. Both are unfiltered and unedited. For this exercise, you'll be freewriting a speech about any one of the scenarios I've listed below. Select one that inspires you, and start writing:

» It's your wedding day. From the perspective of one of your really close friends, write the speech they'd give at your wedding.

» You and your partner are expecting baby #1. One morning as you're brushing your teeth, a wave of emotion washes over you. Standing there in front of the mirror, you are inspired to say a few words to your unborn child.

» You are asked to give a commencement speech to the graduating class at a local university. Standing behind the mic on graduation day, what do you tell them?

| EXERCISE 10 | WATER, SOIL, TREES, AND LEAVES |

In this exercise, you'll be writing 5 different pieces, using 4 lines each. Each poem is about a different theme selected for you. The only rule is that your poems must not be longer than 4 lines. Think back to the peach pit exercise on page 19 for inspiration.

🕐 **Set a timer and spend 2 minutes on each piece:**

1) *Longing is* _____

_____

_____

_____

_____

2) *Fun is* _____

_____

_____

_____

_____

3) *Friendship is* _____

_____

_____

_____

_____

4) *Laughing is* _____

_____

_____

_____

_____

5) *Community is* _____

_____

_____

_____

_____

EXERCISE 11	FIRSTS

Let's take a walk down memory lane. Complete the following prompts in the space provided. If you have never experienced what I've asked you to describe, use your imagination.

1) *My first love*

2) *My first kiss*

3) *My first consensual sexual experience*

4) For the last part of this exercise, you will be writing a spoken word poem. Remember, a spoken word poem is intended to be performed. For a longer description of what spoken word poetry is, revisit page xiv in the introduction.

To get started, select one of the scenarios you wrote about in prompts 1–3. Your selection will be the topic of your piece. Write in stanzas/paragraphs, whatever feels more natural. On the next page, you'll find detailed guidelines for what to write in each of the 4 stanzas/paragraphs. Read the guidelines thoroughly, and refer to them before you begin each of the 4 parts. Turn the page and begin.

GUIDELINES

» **Part One: World Building**

Depending on your topic, begin your piece with one of the following:

» *My first love . . .*

» *My first kiss . . .*

» *My first consensual sexual experience . . .*

For this first paragraph/stanza, describe the experience in brief detail, without describing the emotions. Give us the who, what, where, when, and why. The intention of this first part is to set the scene.

» **Part Two: Emotions**

Begin this section with the words **"It was,"** and write about what the experience felt like. In this second part, you can describe emotions and feelings to whatever extent you like.

» **Part Three: Reflection**

Begin this section with the words **"Before this moment I used to think,"** and write whether your first experience turned out to be exactly how you imagined it would. Did it feel different when it happened? Was it better, or worse?

» **Part Four: Perspective**

Begin this section with the words **"Sitting here today,"** and write about how you feel about this experience from today's vantage point. What's your perspective about all of it now?

🕐 **Set a timer and give yourself 5–7 minutes to write each part.**

LOVING

EXERCISE 12	DROPPING INTO MYSELF

in a world that doesn't consider

my body to be mine

self-pleasure is an act

of self-preservation

when i'm feeling disconnected

i connect with my center

touch by touch

i drop back into myself

at the orgasm

home body, page 74

What joys or shame do you hold on to about masturbation?

EXERCISE 13	CLIMAX

Describe an orgasm, without using the word "orgasm."

EXERCISE 14	INTROSPECTIONS

Writing is exploring. It helps you find answers to difficult questions, and those answers will often surprise you.

Answer each hypothetical question as truthfully as you can:

1) Do you think love alone is enough to make a relationship last, or are elements like money and career integral in the success of a long-term relationship?

2) What are your thoughts on being "crazy in love"? Some say your "soul mate" should make you feel grounded and stable, not "crazy in love," while others say your "soul mate" should make you feel "crazy in love." What do you think?

3) Do you think human beings are meant to be in monogamous relationships, or does monogamy go against our nature?

4) Is cheating forgivable? Why or why not?

5) You have been happily married to the love of your life for 10 years. You have 2 amazing children together. Your partner is your best friend and the both of you have so much fun. One day, you run into a complete stranger at a café and it's love at first sight. You start chatting, you're curious, so you give them your number. You immediately start texting and two weeks later you're convinced this person is your soul mate. If the voice of God said this person was indeed your soul mate, what would you do? Would you end your marriage with your partner whom you still deeply love and pursue a future with this person? Why or why not?

6) Standing in front of you are 2 people:

> »   The first person comes from humble beginnings. Despite the fact that they had no financial support growing up, they managed to pay their way through college. At their current job, they make around $40,000 a year. They aren't expected to make much more than that in their line of work but are happy with this steady income. Although they might not be able to provide you the luxuries you want to experience, they are charming, funny, and you love spending time with them.

> »   The second person is worth hundreds of millions of dollars. They have beautiful homes all over the world. Being with this person would mean being able to do anything your heart desires. You love how powerful and sexy this person is. However, they're a bit mean, narcissistic, and often fail to put you first.

Which would you pick to be your long-term partner and why?

7) If you could redesign dating culture, how would you change it?

the way they
leave
tells you
everything

milk and honey, page 143

CHAPTER THREE

BREAKING

Breakups suck. Hardly anyone gets out of experiencing them at least once, if not many times. I stand in the category of many, and let me tell you, it doesn't matter how many you go through, breakups never get easier.

Heartbreak convinces you that your life is over and you'll never recover. You replay memories in your head, wondering what you could have done differently. You scramble for ways to make it work. It feels like you're grieving a dead thing, except the thing that's dead is the future you two were building. All of it, gone in an instant. It's terrifying.

But time heals, and until it does, keep yourself busy. Sign up for a dance class, make plans with friends, volunteer, find a new hobby. Sure it feels like you'll never get better, but I promise you'll wake up one day and realize you are all you've ever needed.

The exercises in this chapter are based around heartache. Remember, it isn't just romantic relationships that can break your heart. Sometimes it's a friend, a parent, or a dream that didn't work out. No matter who or what it is, you survive and refuse to become the victim of your story.

EXERCISE 1	WOULD YOU RATHER?

Answer the following:

If you had to tell a 5-year-old what heartbreak feels like, what would you say?

EXERCISE 2	SELFISH

In this exercise, you'll be reading my poem "selfish" from *milk and honey*. Two weeks after going through a really bad breakup, which coincidentally ended up being a day before my birthday, I wrote this poem out of deep anger. I was angry that my birthday was in 12 hours and this heartbreak was going to ruin it. I was angry that this guy got what he wanted and left. I wanted to rip my hair out, or maybe, I wanted to rip out his.

The day that I wrote it, I was sitting in the passenger's seat of my cousin's car and we were pulling out of the grocery store parking lot when this feeling came over me. Elizabeth Gilbert calls this feeling "big magic." It's when creativity suddenly takes over your body and the magic flows out of you effortlessly. It allows you to create with so much ease, you believe you were born for it. These moments don't happen often, but when they do, it's magnificent.

That day I felt "big magic," pulled out my iPhone 5, and began typing furiously into the notes app. As I pressed the screen with my thumbs, I felt a beautiful rage. A rage that made me feel like I was stepping into my strength and becoming the giant I was meant to be. Once or twice my cousin tried to make conversation and I impatiently snapped at him to be quiet. Luckily, he'd witnessed me in a state of "big magic" before, so he took no offense and obliged. The drive home was only 7 minutes long and by the end of it I'd written multiple pages.

When we pulled into the house, my heart was racing. I don't remember my cousin leaving the car, getting out the groceries, or taking them inside. I do remember punching in the last line of the poem and feeling *glorious*.

In the next few pages you will be reading and workshopping this poem. For the purposes of this exercise, I've divided it into 3 sections. In between each section I've left space for you to write. In this space you'll be writing new stanzas for the poem. Remember, it's a freewriting exercise, so it doesn't matter if your additions make the poem "confusing" or "messy." That's the point. I want to see what your unfiltered rage looks like on the page, the same way mine did when I first wrote this poem.

GUIDELINES

» Before you start writing, read through all 3 sections of the poem from beginning to end.

» Then return to the beginning, reread the first section to inspire your freewriting for the first block of blank space, and write what comes to you.

» Once you've finished writing in the first block of space, reread everything prior to that, and let it inspire your freewrite for the second block.

» Once you've finished writing in the second block of space, reread everything prior to that, and let it inspire your freewrite for the third block.

Turn the page to begin the exercise.

i will tell you about selfish people. even when they know they will hurt you they walk into your life to taste you because you are the type of being they don't want to miss out on. you are too much shine to not be felt. so when they have gotten a good look at everything you have to offer. when they have taken your skin your hair your secrets with them. when they realize how real this is. how much of a storm you are and it hits them.

that is when the cowardice sets in. that is when the person you thought they were is replaced by the sad reality of what they are. that is when they lose every fighting bone in their body and leave after saying *you will find better than me.*

you will stand there naked with half of them still hidden
somewhere inside you and sob. asking them why they did it.
why they forced you to love them when they had no intention
of loving you back and they'll say something along the lines of
i just had to try. i had to give it a chance. it was you after all.

but that isn't romantic. it isn't sweet. the idea that they were
so engulfed by your existence they had to risk breaking it for
the sake of knowing they weren't the one missing out. your
existence meant that little next to their curiosity of you.

that is the thing about selfish people. they gamble entire beings.
entire souls to please their own. one second they are holding
you like the world in their lap and the next they have belittled
you to a mere picture. a moment. something of the past. one
second. they swallow you up and whisper they want to spend
the rest of their life with you. but the moment they sense fear.
they are already halfway out the door. without having the nerve
to let you go with grace. as if the human heart means that little
to them.

and after all this. after all of the taking. the nerve. isn't it sad
and funny how people have more guts these days to undress you
with their fingers than they do to pick up the phone and call.
apologize. for the loss. and this is how you lose her.

- selfish

milk and honey, pages 140–141

EXERCISE 3	THE TO-DO LIST

Here's a list poem from *milk and honey*:

> to do list (after the breakup):
>   1. take refuge in your bed.
>   2. cry. till the tears stop (this will take a few days).
>   3. don't listen to slow songs.
>   4. delete their number from your phone even though
>   it is memorized on your fingertips.
>   5. don't look at old photos.
>   6. find the closest ice cream shop and treat yourself
>   to two scoops of mint chocolate chip. the mint will
>   calm your heart. you deserve the chocolate.
>   7. buy new bed sheets.
>   8. collect all the gifts, t-shirts, and everything with their smell
>   on it and drop it off at a donation center.
>   9. plan a trip.
> 10. perfect the art of smiling and nodding
>   when someone brings their name up in conversation.
> 11. start a new project.
> 12. whatever you do. do not call.
> 13. do not beg for what does not want to stay.
> 14. stop crying at some point.
> 15. allow yourself to feel foolish for believing
>   you could've built the rest of your life
>   in someone else's stomach.
> 16. breathe.

milk and honey, page 142

For this exercise, you will be writing your own to-do list. However, your list poem will be about a "list of things to do in times of sadness."

GUIDELINES

» Avoid using the items on my list—come up with your own.

» Remember to freewrite! Unfiltered and uncensored energy only please 😃.

» Your list can be as long as you'd like.

Turn the page and begin.

To-do list in times of sadness:

»

»

»

»

»

»

»

»

»

»

»

»

»

EXERCISE 4	**IDEA VS. REALITY**

did you think i was a city

big enough for a weekend getaway

i am the town surrounding it

the one you've never heard of

but always pass through

there are no neon lights here

no skyscrapers or statues

but there is thunder

for i make bridges tremble

i am not street meat i am homemade jam

thick enough to cut the sweetest

thing your lips will touch

i am not police sirens

i am the crackle of a fireplace

i'd burn you and you still

couldn't take your eyes off me

cause i'd look so beautiful doing it

you'd blush

i am not a hotel room i am home

i am not the whiskey you want

i am the water you need

don't come here with expectations

and try to make a vacation out of me

milk and honey, page 97

Isn't it *hilarious* the number of excuses we make for someone we want to be romantically involved with? We can become so distracted by our own feelings, we don't see the person they are; all we see is our projected idea of them. This idea can become so powerful we start ignoring red flags. We think that our love for them will be strong enough to inspire change. In the end, we have to let go and accept reality.

After a relationship like this, I often make mental lists of what ideas I projected onto the person—all of the narratives I made up about them based on my feelings. Then, I compare that list with their actions, because it's their actions that illustrate reality. This "idea" versus "reality" comparison helps me get over them faster. It helps to know that most of what I was in love with was never *really* there.

I'm not sure why we project such narratives onto people. Maybe it's human nature. Maybe it's the fairy tales we read as children or the romantic comedies we watched growing up.

For this exercise, I want you to refer back to an old relationship, friendship, or unrequited love and fill in the chart with your "ideas of them" versus the "reality."

GUIDELINES

» First, fill out the "my idea of them" column with all the false ideas and narratives you had about the person.

» After you've completed the "my idea of them" column, start filling in the "reality" column row by row.

» You don't need to fill out all 10 rows; fill in however many you can.

» I've provided you with an example to help you get started.

	MY IDEA OF THEM	VS.	REALITY
1	I thought he was a warm and kind person because he was warm and kind to me.	VS.	I discovered that he wasn't as kind as I thought. He often judged and made mean comments about people he didn't know. I ignored this because I wanted him to be "the one" so badly.
2		VS.	

	MY IDEA OF THEM	VS.	REALITY
3		VS.	
4		VS.	
5		VS.	
6		VS.	

	MY IDEA OF THEM	VS.	REALITY
7		VS.	
8		VS.	
9		VS.	
10		VS.	

| EXERCISE 5 | WHEN YOU CAN SEE IT SO CLEARLY BUT THE OTHER PERSON DOESN'T |

you said. if it is meant to be. fate will bring us back
together. for a second i wonder if you are really
that naive. if you really believe fate works like
that. as if it lives in the sky staring down at us. as
if it has five fingers and spends its time placing us
like pieces of chess. as if it is not the choices we
make. who taught you that. tell me. who
convinced you. you've been given a heart and
a mind that isn't yours to use. that your actions
do not define what will become of you. i want to
scream and shout *it's us you fool. we're the only*
ones that can bring us back together. but
instead i sit quietly. smiling softly through
quivering lips thinking. isn't it such a tragic thing.
when you can see it so clearly but the other person
doesn't.

milk and honey, page 84

Isn't it interesting how two people can perceive a single situation so differently?

For this exercise, reflect on a situation between any relationship you've had with a partner, parent, friend, or coworker, where the two of you saw the same situation in two different ways. What were the differences in perception and how did they make you feel?

I've provided you with a prompt to begin:

We were looking at

EXERCISE 6	FALSEHOODS

you were the most beautiful thing i'd ever felt till
now. and i was convinced you'd remain the most
beautiful thing i'd ever feel. do you know how
limiting that is. to think at such a ripe young age i'd
experienced the most exhilarating person i'd ever
meet. how i'd spend the rest of my life just settling.
to think i'd tasted the rawest form of honey and
everything else would be refined and synthetic. that
nothing beyond this point would add up. that all the
years beyond me could not combine themselves to
be sweeter than you.

- falsehood

milk and honey, page 108

What a tragic thought—to think that by my early 20s I'd felt the greatest love I'd
ever feel and no one else would love me that way.

Was I desperate to want this person so badly? Was I insecure? Did I not have self-
worth? Maybe I held on to toxic relationships because I didn't know any better. When
you grow up in high-stress environments, feeling highly stressed tends to be your
resting state. Someone who grows up in a healthy environment might recognize a toxic
relationship as a warning sign and leave. But for someone whose resting state is anxiety,
a toxic relationship can feel normal, and then all it takes is one asshole giving you a bit
of attention and suddenly you think you've found "the one."

I wrote this poem while trying to convince myself that even though every cell in my
body was pining for him, he wasn't right for me. Regardless of whether I believed it or
not, I told myself I *would* find love again, and *that* love would be happier and healthier.

I wrote this poem when I was 20-years-old, and it was published in *milk and honey*. By the time I was 24-years-old and publishing *the sun and her flowers*, reading this poem felt like I was reading somebody else's experience. The 24-year-old version of me didn't recognize the 20-year-old version who thought she'd already experienced the most exhilarating person she'd ever meet. There had been so much growth in those 4 years. This isn't to say that the 20-year-old had it wrong—it was just a different perception at a different age. It's incredible how time can change how we perceive situations. If I was asked to write a new version of this poem today, it would probably go something like:

> you will not be the most beautiful thing i'll ever feel
>
> there are decades of greatness ahead of me
>
> i won't lessen my shine to give you credit
>
> my life has just started
>
> i can't wait to get out there
>
> and taste the rest of it

> *- falsehood 2.0*

See the difference in perspective? I love revisiting old poems to see how much I've grown.

In this exercise, you will write a prose poem in 2 paragraphs.

In the first paragraph, revisit a moment in your life where you lost something and felt you'd never experience anything as great again. Write about what falsehood you were convinced of and why.

For the second paragraph, write from today's perspective about how that falsehood was incorrect. How do you see that situation now? How have you grown?

I've provided you with a prompt to start each paragraph.

Set a timer for 15 minutes and begin.

I was convinced that

Now I realize that

EXERCISE 7	WHAT I DIDN'T KNOW

what i miss most is how you loved me. but what i didn't
know was how you loved me had so much to do with
the person i was. it was a reflection of everything i gave
to you. coming back to me. how did i not see that. how.
did i sit here soaking in the idea that no one else would
love me that way. when it was i who taught you. when it
was i who showed you how to fill. the way i needed to be
filled. how cruel i was to myself. giving you credit for my
warmth simply because you had felt it. thinking it was
you who gave me strength. wit. beauty. simply because
you recognized it. as if i was already not these things
before i met you. as if i did not remain all these once you
left.

milk and honey, page 138

Yesss!!!! This is the badass version of me that picks up the moping version of me and says, "Let's go, we're gonna fight everrrrrrybody and their mom." I freakin' love that version of me. She lets me cry, complain, feel sorry for myself, and then lifts me out of my misery.

I call this poem my redemption poem. Half the poem is me talking about allllll the things I thought I lost, while the second half is a realization of how I didn't lose shit.

For this exercise, you're going to write your own redemption poem. Like mine, yours will have 2 parts.

GUIDELINES

» Think about something you felt you lost after someone walked out of your life. That something will be the topic of your piece.

» Start your piece by writing about what you thought you lost. Why and how did it feel to think you'd lost it?

» Before you begin the second part of the piece, think about what you'd tell your best friend if they felt this way. You'd probably grab them by the shoulders to shake them until they realized how incredible they are. What would you tell them to make them feel better? Now respond to yourself in the same way.

Set a timer for 15 minutes and begin freewriting:

| EXERCISE 8 | WOULD YOU RATHER? |

Would you rather be broken up with or be the one breaking up with someone?

EXERCISE 9	WHAT AM I?

Take some time to examine the following drawing:

Now, write about what this drawing brings up for you. What was the first thing that you thought of when you observed it? Does the drawing have a story? What is it trying to communicate?

🕐 **Set a timer for 10 minutes and begin:**

EXERCISE 10	DO NOT BE THE VICTIM OF YOUR OWN STORY

🕐 **Answer the following question by setting a timer for 15 minutes and begin freewriting:**

In what ways could you take more responsibility over your life?

EXERCISE 11	FORGIVENESS

⏱ **Set a timer for 10 minutes, read the following question, and begin freewriting:**

Who do you need to forgive and is there a reason you haven't forgiven them?

EXERCISE 12	GREATEST LESSONS

As much as it sucks, and as much as I hope to *never* experience it again, heartbreak teaches us important lessons. In your opinion, what are the greatest lessons you've learned from heartbreak? Complete this exercise in paragraphs, stanzas, or as a list poem.

⏱ **Set a timer for 10 minutes and begin freewriting:**

EXERCISE 13	RESPONSIBILITY

⏱ **Set a timer for 15 minutes, read the following question, and begin freewriting:**

How have you hurt other people?

EXERCISE 14	DATE YOURSELF

you must enter a relationship

with yourself

before anyone else

milk and honey, page 150

🕐 **Set a timer for 20 minutes and answer the following questions:**

1) What would entering a healthier relationship with yourself look like?

2) I have a friend who's always wanted a dude to buy her a diamond ring. After her last boyfriend cheated on her, she realized waiting for a man to buy her a ring was pointless. She could very well get one for herself, so she got herself a diamond.

I have another friend who's happily single and just celebrated her 40th birthday. The one thing she wanted more than anything else was to have a baby. However, she didn't see herself getting into a serious relationship anytime soon and decided that becoming a mother shouldn't depend on her finding a partner. The two didn't have to be mutually exclusive. She's now the single mother of a beautiful baby boy.

Some of my other friends have bought their first homes on their own. Others buy themselves flowers and take themselves out for dinner once a week.

What are some things you've always wanted a partner to do for you, that you could do for yourself?

| EXERCISE 15 | NOT YOUR BEST MOMENTS |

Answer the following as truthfully as you can. Set a timer for 15 minutes and begin freewriting:

Have you ever led someone on because they were nice to you and checked all your boxes?

EXERCISE 16	THE BRIDGE

Throughout most of this chapter we've been exploring romantic heartbreak. For this exercise, let's shake things up.

Close your eyes and take some deep breaths. Some days I need to breathe for 5 minutes to feel grounded. Other days I need to breathe for 20. Once you feel grounded, open your eyes, go to the next page, and get started.

1) Draw what "broken" feels like:

2) Draw what "healed" feels like:

3) In jot form, note the differences and similarities between your two drawings.

» Differences between the two drawings:

» Similarities (if any) between the two drawings:

» Other observations:

4) In the drawing portion of this exercise, you explored the concept of being broken and healed. Now, for the writing portion, you're going to explore what happens between the two: the journey of going from "broken" to "healed." What is this journey like? Pull inspiration from moments you had to pick yourself up during tough times and move forward.

Refer to your drawings and notes from parts 1–3 to help you write. I've given you a prompt to help you get started.

⏱ Set a timer for 15 minutes and begin freewriting:

The in-between is strange.
It is an awakening from how I saw,
to how I will see.

| EXERCISE 17 | I HAVE BEEN LOOKING FOR YOU |

Pick any individual person from your past or present, someone you hope to meet, or someone living or dead.

For this exercise, you'll be writing a letter to this individual using all 10 words I've provided in the word bank on the following page.

GUIDELINES

» Have a timer ready. Once you read the prompt, start the timer and begin freewriting.

» When the timer hits **2 minutes,** refer to the first word listed in the word bank provided on the following page and incorporate it into your writing right then and there. After you've incorporated it, keep writing.

» When your timer hits **4 minutes,** refer to the second word on the list and incorporate it into your writing. After you've incorporated it, continue freewriting.

» When your timer hits **6 minutes,** include the third word. When your timer hits **8 minutes,** include the fourth word, so on and so forth, until all 10 words have been used and you've concluded the piece to your liking.

This exercise should take **22 minutes** to complete. You're essentially spending the first 2 minutes starting your letter off with the prompt I've provided, and spending 2 minutes on each of the 10 words after that.

🕐 **Set a timer for 22 minutes, take a deep breath, and begin freewriting:**

Word Bank

1. Chair (include after 2 minutes)
2. Flower (include after 4 minutes)
3. Salt (include after 6 minutes)
4. Clock (include after 8 minutes)
5. Running (include after 10 minutes)
6. Traffic (include after 12 minutes)
7. Yellow (include after 14 minutes)
8. Cotton (include after 16 minutes)
9. Fingernails (include after 18 minutes)
10. Tornado (include after 20 minutes)

Dear _____ .

It has been a long time coming. I have been looking for you.

EXERCISE 18	CIRCLE POEM

A circle poem is a poem that starts and ends with either the exact or some variation of the same words, lines, or phrases. Here's an old circle poem I wrote:

> i broke up with the person i love
>
> left my friendships behind
>
> moved cities
>
> but i still woke up
>
> in the dark
>
> turns out you can run away from your life
>
> but sadness is like a shadow
>
> it follows you everywhere
>
> the next day when
>
> i woke up
>
> i moved back to my city
>
> made up with all my friends
>
> and kissed the person i love

Note how I ended the poem (lines 10–13) is similar to how I started it (lines 1–4). That callback makes this a circle poem.

Lines 1–4 read:

> i broke up with the person i love
>
> left my friendships behind
>
> moved cities
>
> but i still woke up

Lines 10–13 read:

> i woke up
>
> i moved back to my city
>
> made up with all my friends
>
> and kissed the person i love

The beginning and end of your circle poem doesn't have to be *exactly* the same—it just has to be close enough for the repitition to be recognizable.

I enjoy writing and reading circle poems because they have a nice rhythm to them. I love when things come full circle. For this exercise, you'll be writing your own circle poem.

1) To get started, write down one habit that you wish you could get rid of:

Your poem will start off with the words:

I'd like to stop _____

(the habit you wish you could get rid of)

Because you're writing a circle poem, the last few lines must be similar to the first few. Remember to make that callback. I've provided you with prompts to help you get started.

For this exercise, write in the bolded lines only.

🕐 **Set a timer for 15 minutes and begin freewriting:**

I'd like to stop _____

It's so _____

_____

_____

_____

_____

_____

_____

_____

_____

It's so _____

I'd like to stop _____

2) Let's try another:

Pick someone you've had a crush on or dated in the past. If no one comes to mind, use your imagination. Then, fill in the blanks by writing about your experience with them.

⏱ Set a timer for 10 minutes and begin freewriting:

Can you believe we _____

That was _____

_____

_____

_____

_____

_____

_____

_____

_____

_____

That was _____

Can you believe we _____

3) Now write a circle poem about any topic of your choice without any prompts from me.

🕐 **Set a timer for 15 minutes and begin freewriting:**

EXERCISE 19	FULFILLING MY OWN DREAMS

We grew up bombarded with unrealistic images of love. We now spend more time finding "the one" than we do building a bond with ourselves.

Luckily, many of us have learned that another person can't complete us; only we have the power to do that. The answers we are looking for are within us.

For this exercise, write about how you can shift more of your energy into developing a stronger bond with yourself. How can you feel more at ease in your body? What do you hope to gain from a partner that you could gain on your own?

🕐 **Set a timer for 15 minutes and begin freewriting:**

EXERCISE 20	STRUGGLE

For this exercise, you will be writing a spoken word poem, 5 paragraphs/stanzas long, about anything you're currently struggling with right now.

GUIDELINES

» Start your timer and begin freewriting the first paragraph/stanza using the words **"We met."** Drop clues, but do not reveal the struggle you're referring to. You can write about where and when you met this struggle, and where your relationship with it began. Spend **4 minutes** setting the scene.

» When the timer hits 4 minutes, move on to the second paragraph/stanza with the words **"And here you are."** Continue to be discreet about *exactly* what your struggle is. Instead, write about it in greater detail. What does it look like? Does it have a physical body? Does it have a smell? What does it feel like? Do you have a nickname for it? What makes the struggle strong or weak? The details in this second part should make the reader feel the weight of your struggle. Spend **4 minutes** writing this part.

» When the timer hits 8 minutes, start your third paragraph/stanza by revealing your struggle. Tell the reader what it is, and then write what you'd say to this struggle if you could have a conversation with it. How would it feel to say these things? Spend **4 minutes** writing this part.

» When the timer hits 12 minutes, move on to the fourth paragraph/stanza. Imagine yourself overcoming this struggle and write about what this victory feels like. Spend **4 minutes** writing this part.

» When the timer hits 16 minutes, move on to the fifth paragraph/stanza. To conclude the exercise, write about what you can do now that the struggle isn't holding you back. What's next for you? Spend **4 minutes** writing this part.

» Wrap up your piece at the **20-minute** mark.

Set a timer for 20 minutes and begin freewriting:

EXERCISE 21	ROUND OF APPLAUSE

Complete the following in jot form:

Write a list of reasons why you are an ideal friend or partner.

»

»

»

»

»

»

»

»

»

»

»

»

»

»

»

»

»

»

»

»

»

»

i thank the universe
for taking
everything it has taken
and giving to me
everything it is giving

- *balance*

milk and honey, page 159

CHAPTER FOUR

HEALING

Healing is to wake up every morning and dedicate yourself to yourself. It is a practice that has no end or finish line. It is never complete. It will remain a work in progress as long as you walk this Earth. Healing is reaching out to ask for help however many times you need it. Having the courage to take care of yourself. Healing is never linear. Healing is breakdowns. Being compassionate. Knowing that even at your best, there will be downward spirals. Healing is bringing all of yourself to the table and saying *I probably have no idea what I'm doing, but I'm still going to try.* Healing is beginning where you are. It is falling off the practice and getting back up knowing nothing was lost. No one gets through life without scars. Everyone is doing their best with what they have. To be human is to be imperfect. So go easy. Be kind to yourself and each other.

| EXERCISE 1 | A LIST OF THINGS TO HEAL YOUR MOOD |

Below is a list poem from my third book, *home body*. It's about the different things I do to make myself feel better when I'm having a rough day. I have this poem taped to my bathroom mirror as a reminder that I am more powerful than I sometimes believe.

list of things to heal your mood:

1) cry it. walk it. write it. scream it.

   dance it out of your body.

2) if after all that

   you are still

   spiraling out of control

   ask yourself if sinking into the mud is worth it

3) the answer is no

4) the answer is breathe

5) sip tea and feel your nervous system settle

6) you are the hero of your life

7) this feeling doesn't have power over you

8) the universe has prepared you to handle this

9) no matter how dark it gets

   the light is always on its way

10) you are the light

11) walk yourself back to where the love lives

home body, page 35

For the first exercise of this chapter, re-create this poem by writing your own "list of things to heal my mood." The only rule is you can't use anything from my list.

🕐 **Set a timer for 10 minutes and begin freewriting:**

list of things to heal my mood:

1)

2)

3)

4)

5)

6)

7)

8)

9)

10)

11)

EXERCISE 2	PRIVATE

🕐 **Set a timer for 15 minutes and answer the following:**

Who are you when no one is looking?

EXERCISE 3	COMPASSION

Compassion is our ability to recognize the suffering of others and feel a desire to help them. Most of us are pretty good at being compassionate toward others. We are gentle, kind, and patient with them because we know that's what they need.

Why are we so good at having compassion for others but terrible at having it for ourselves? When we're suffering, we quickly come to the conclusion that we must be weak. Rather than being kind, our natural response can be mean and impatient.

In this exercise, you will examine your relationship with self-compassion.

1) How often are you able to have compassion for yourself? Circle below:

1.	2.	3.	4.	5.
Never	Rarely	Sometimes	Often	Always

2) Why is having compassion for yourself so difficult/easy?

3) Imagine you have a lot of compassion for yourself and you treat yourself like you would your best friend. You are gentle, forgiving, and don't blame yourself for circumstances outside of your control.

What does this compassionate dialogue sound like?

| EXERCISE 4 | GIVE YOURSELF SOME CREDIT |

🕐 **Set a timer for 20 minutes and begin freewriting your answers to the following questions:**

How are you brave?

In what ways are you intelligent?

How are you powerful?

EXERCISE 5	SEEING YOURSELF

today i saw myself for the first time

when i dusted off

the mirror of my mind

and the woman looking back

took my breath away

who was this beautiful beastling

this extra-celestial earthling

i touched my face and my reflection

touched the woman of my dreams

all her gorgeous smirking back at me

my knees surrendered to the earth

as i wept and sighed at how

i'd gone my whole life

being myself

but not seeing myself

spent decades living inside my body

never left it once

yet managed to miss all its miracles

isn't it funny how you can

occupy a space without

being in touch with it

how it took so long for me

to open the eyes of my eyes

embrace the heart of my heart

kiss the soles of my swollen feet

and hear them whisper

thank you

thank you

thank you

for noticing

home body, page 152

When insecurities fall off our shoulders and we start to see ourselves, it feels glorious and transcendent. Imagine you're in that state of transcendence right now, with access to endless power and self-love. What does it feel like to have those insecurities slide off your shoulders, fall to the floor, and never be seen again?

The prompts in this exercise have been pulled from my poem above.

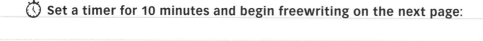 **Set a timer for 10 minutes and begin freewriting on the next page:**

today i saw myself for the first time when _____

_____

_____

_____

_____

_____

_____

_____

i wept and sighed at how _____

_____

_____

_____

_____

_____

_____

_____

it's funny how _____

_____

_____

_____

_____

_____

_____

_____

EXERCISE 6	ROOM

You're standing in front of a closed door. You turn the doorknob and step into a mostly empty room except for two chairs in the center, facing each other. One of the chairs is occupied. You take a seat in the empty chair and sitting in front of you is your 15-year-old self. You reach out and hold their hands.

A list of 14 questions appears on the following page. In the space provided, answer them in order with a single sentence response (if you end up writing a sentence or two more, that's okay, but try to keep it concise). Spend around 1 minute answering each question.

Don't read all the questions before you begin. In sequential order, read one question, write your answer, then move on to the next question and do the same.

If you'd like, use a timer to keep track of how long you're spending on each line.

 **Set a timer for 14 minutes and begin freewriting:**

1) What's the first thing you notice when you sit down and look into the eyes of your 15-year-old self?

2) What are they wearing?

3) Describe the atmosphere of the room, literally or figuratively (i.e., is it dark, light, tiled, hardwood, well-lit, scary, warm?).

4) Was it you who called this meeting or was it them?

5) The 15-year-old version of you is the first to break the silence. They ask you a question. What do they ask?

6) How do you respond?

7) What else do the two of you talk about?

8) How does the conversation make you feel?

9) Does this conversation change anything for you?

10) It's time for you to go. What are your last words to your 15-year-old self?

11) You get up, give your 15-year-old self a hug, and they whisper something in your ear. What do they say?

12) They take your hand and place something in it. Without looking at what it is, you walk toward the door. What's the last thought you have before stepping out?

13) With the door shut behind you, you open your hand to see what they gave. What is it?

14) Where are you off to next?

EXERCISE 7	LOVE YOURSELF

🕐 **Set a timer for 10 minutes and begin freewriting:**

Why are you worthy of joy?

| EXERCISE 8 | A MOVIE ABOUT MY LIFE |

You are approached by a renowned film director who wants to make a movie about your life. You accept their offer.

1) In one paragraph, describe the general plot of the movie:

The director loves the plot, and the movie goes into production. Fast-forward a few months, and you're sitting front row on premiere night. The theater is packed. The lights dim, and the movie begins.

2) The opening scene of the film is you standing in a hallway. Given the plot of the film, where are you and why?

3) Describe the emotions your character feels in this opening scene:

4) Does your character face any problems or challenges?

5) What's your favorite part of the film?

6) Describe the closing scene:

EXERCISE 9	LEAF

When I'm having a rough day, I try to be out in nature. Walking, hiking, or having a picnic always helps my mood. I imagine how peaceful it must be to be a tree, leaf, or stream of water. Being close to nature always lifts my mood. It reminds me of how miraculous the Earth is, and how lucky we are to simply be alive.

For this exercise, imagine that you're a leaf on a tree, and what that would feel like. Answer questions 1–15 in their given order.

Don't read all the questions at once. Start by reading the first, answering it, then read the second, answer that, then the third, and so on.

Don't think too long and hard on your answers—write the first thought that comes to mind. Try your best to keep your answers between 2–3 sentences.

Before you start, take a minute to close your eyes and embody the leaf. Imagine the experience using all of your senses. Once you begin to embody the leaf, get started.

1) What does your skin feel like?

2) What kind of tree are you attached to (i.e., describe its appearance or location)?

3) Are you isolated or is there a lot going on around you?

4) Do you like your tree? Why?

5) How does it feel when people walk by and don't notice you?

6) How does it feel to be noticed?

7) In general, what are your thoughts on human beings?

8) What does the wind feel like when it hits your back?

9) When the wind lifts you off your tree and takes you dancing, what do you say to it?

10) Do you like losing control?

11) Finish this sentence: *The wind takes me to . . .*

12) Where is this new destination and why has the wind brought you here?

13) Do you miss being on your tree?

14) If you had one wish, what would it be?

15) Any last words?

EXERCISE 10	FREE YOURSELF

Forgiving others is freeing yourself. And you, my darling, deserve to be free. It takes a lot to forgive those who've wronged us. You may not be ready to forgive some of those people and that's perfectly okay. However, practicing forgiveness privately can help us imagine a future where forgiveness is possible.

In this exercise, you'll be practicing forgiveness to see what it feels like.

1) I forgive _____ for

2) I forgive _____ for

3) I forgive _____ for

4) I forgive _____ for

5) I forgive _____ for

| EXERCISE 11 | **EXTEND** |

Return to the previous exercise and select one of the individuals you forgave. Imagine you forgive this person in real life. In an ideal world, how would you want this scenario to play out? What would you want them to respond with?

🕐 **Set a timer for 15 minutes and begin freewriting:**

EXERCISE 12	MOVING FORWARD

🕐 **Set a timer for 10 minutes and answer the following:**

Why is forgiveness important?

EXERCISE 13	TO THE MEN IN MY FAMILY

⏱ **Set a timer for 15 minutes, read the prompt, and begin freewriting:**

If I could sit with all the men in my lineage, I would tell them

| EXERCISE 14 | GET TO THE ROOT |

to heal
you have to
get to the root
of the wound
and kiss it all the way up

the sun and her flowers, page 235

1) The poem above is from my second book, *the sun and her flowers*. The illustration below accompanies the poem. For the purpose of this exercise, I've given it four labels: **center**, **petal**, **stem**, and **root**. In jot form, answer the question written under each label:

center
What is a mental, physical, or emotional wound you carry?

petal
In your day-to-day, how do you hide this wound from the world?

stem
How far back does this wound extend?

root
At its inception, how do you think the wound formed?

2) This illustration and poem illustrates how:

»   we all have wounds.

»   we try to hide these wounds from the world.

»   we must get to the root of our wounds if we want to heal them. Often, these roots reach back to our childhoods.

For the last part of this exercise, I want you to write about the wound you uncovered in part 1. Your piece will be 5 paragraphs/stanzas long—write in whatever format suits you. Each of the 5 paragraphs/stanzas should expand on your answers in part 1. Here's what you'll be writing in each of the 5 parts:

GUIDELINES

»   *Part 1: center*
🕐 **Set a timer for 3 minutes** and start by introducing the mental, emotional, or physical wound you uncovered under the "center" label of the illustration. At the 3-minute mark, stop writing and move on to the next section.

»   *Part 2: petal*
This section is called "petal" because petals surround the center of the flower to protect what's inside. 🕐 **Set a timer for 5 minutes** and write about how you try to hide this wound from the world. At the 5-minute mark, stop writing and move on to the next section.

»   *Part 3: stem*
🕐 **Set a timer for 3 minutes** and write about how long you've had this wound. How far back in your life does the wound extend? At the 3-minute mark, stop writing and move on to the next section.

»   *Part 4: root*
🕐 **Set a timer for 5 minutes** and determine when this wound was formed. What is the original root? Stop writing at the 5-minute mark and move on to the next section.

»   *Part 5:*
🕐 **Set a timer for 5 minutes** and write about what it would take to heal this wound. How can you start this journey? Stop writing at the 5-minute mark.

EXERCISE 15	POWER

🕐 **Set a timer for 10 minutes and complete the following thought:**

The women in my life have done

EXERCISE 16	MIND, BODY, AND I

"Today I am thanking my body for keeping us going. For being here when I wasn't."

I wrote this passage in my journal when I realized how my **mind**, **body**, and **I** ("**I**" being my spirit) all exist in one place but often feel disconnected from each other.

For example, when it's anxious, my **mind** fills me up with fears and doubts.

This worries me and **I** become so terrified of the lies my **mind** tells me **I** start to disassociate from my **body** to lessen the fear.

But no matter how much **I** disconnect from or neglect it, my **body** continues breathing and beating to keep me alive. Whether my **mind** and **I** show up for it or not, my **body** shows up for us.

Before you start this exercise, find a quiet spot, have a seat, and take 10 deep breaths with your eyes closed.

Starting at your feet, scan your body. Feel into each part: to the ankles, up the calves, then the knees, the thighs, and abdomen. Then move up to your belly, heart, neck, face, and crown of the head.

When you get to the crown of the head, become aware of your mind. Listen to what it's saying.

Feel how the thoughts affect you.

After about 5 minutes of this meditation, read the exercise guidelines and begin freewriting.

GUIDELINES

» Write a 3-part piece (using paragraphs/stanzas) about your "**mind**, **body**, and **I**" (the "**I**" refers to your spirit). The goal of this exercise is to hone in on what your "**mind**, **body**, and **I**" are trying to communicate.

» *Part 1: Mind*
We may not realize it, but we spend a lot of time thinking the same thoughts over and over again. These recurring thoughts shape our experience of the world. What are some recurring thoughts you have? ⏱ **Set a timer and complete this part within 4 minutes.**

» *Part 2: I*
How do your recurring thoughts impact you? Are they amplifying or limiting your experiences of the world? Are you and your mind both at ease with one another, or is there conflict? ⏱ **Set a timer and complete this part within 4 minutes.**

» *Part 3: Body*
While your mind is thinking away, and you are being affected by those thoughts, what is your body feeling? ⏱ **Set a timer and complete this part within 4 minutes.**

EXERCISE 17	PLAY

The older we get, the less we seem to play. With all the energy our careers and other responsibilities consume, having fun can become difficult.

I've often struggled to have fun because I was convinced I didn't have time to do things that didn't directly help me accomplish my goals. I felt this need to hustle nonstop, which left no room for play. I was obsessed with optimizing every hour of my day, and only doing things that were productive. All of this eventually led to burnout until I learned that having fun is just as important, if not more, than working. In fact, having fun actually plays a big part in how productive we are. The more balance we have, the longer we can sustain ourselves.

🕐 **Set a timer for 10 minutes and answer the following:**

How can you start having more fun?

EXERCISE 18	THE WOMEN IN MY LINEAGE

🕐 **Set a timer for 15 minutes and freewrite the following:**

If you could ask your grandmother, great-grandmother, and all the women who came before you any question(s), what would you ask and why?

EXERCISE 19	PRETTY

i want to apologize to all the women
i have called pretty
before i've called them intelligent or brave
i am sorry i made it sound as though
something as simple as what you're born with
is the most you have to be proud of when your
spirit has crushed mountains
from now on i will say things like
you are resilient or *you are extraordinary*
not because i don't think you're pretty
but because you are so much more than that

milk and honey, page 179

The year was 2013. Long before I wrote it, the lines of this poem replayed in my head like a song on repeat. This went on for months. Instead of writing the poem down, I ignored it because I thought it was corny.

But the poem didn't care. It replayed in my head over and over again until I got so annoyed I wrote it down in the hopes of getting it out of my system.

It seamlessly flowed out of me in 11 lines. Once it was on paper, I felt relieved. Then, I was about to turn the page and start working on something else, but the poem wouldn't let me. I don't know why, but I was overcome with this odd confidence and felt compelled to share the poem online. I made a few edits, published it, and the reaction from my readers was astounding.

I couldn't believe it. This poem had been knocking at my door for months and I'd flat-out ignored it. Now it was being read and shared nonstop and to this day it remains one of my most popular pieces.

I think about this whenever I go into a writing session because it's proof that we often get in our own way. Sometimes we stop our flow because we become resistant and start overthinking. Our gut tries to guide us into beautiful directions, but we think we know better. Maybe we think people will laugh at our innermost thoughts. Maybe we don't want to give up control. But if we're trying to be authentic, we've got to let go and follow our instincts.

Read the poem on the previous page again and use it as inspiration to write your own apology to women. Your apology can be personal and specific to one woman or more general to women as a whole. To help you get started, I've provided you with prompts directly from my poem.

1)

i want to apologize to all the women _____

_____

_____

_____

from now on i will _____

_____

_____

_____

because women are so much more than that

2) Women have been globally oppressed for thousands of years regardless of class, caste, country, or race, so one apology poem isn't enough. We've got a lot of healing to do, and apologies are necessary for healing to occur, so let's write a few more.

i want to apologize to all the women _____

_____

_____

_____

from now on i will _____

_____

_____

_____

because women are so much more than that

3)

i want to apologize to all the women _____

_____

_____

_____

from now on i will _____

_____

_____

_____

because women are so much more than that

4)

i want to apologize to all the women _____

_____

_____

_____

from now on i will _____

_____

_____

_____

because women are so much more than that

EXERCISE 20	MEDITATION

In recent years, meditation has become a part of my writing process. I begin each writing session by sitting on the floor and doing breathing exercises. Depending on how I feel, I stretch, do yoga, or sit in silence, aware of what thoughts are coming and going.

Meditating is a grounding experience. It makes me feel settled, which is a great mental space to be in before writing.

For this exercise, I thought it would be nice to explore gratitude. You've probably done some form of this exercise before, but you can never be too grateful. Gratitude is a lot like gravity—it helps us stay grounded and centered.

1) Fill in the blanks below with all the things you're grateful for:

I am grateful for

I am grateful for

I am grateful for

I am grateful for

I am grateful for

I am grateful for

I am grateful for

I am grateful for

I am grateful for

I am grateful for

Tonglen is a Buddhist form of meditation. The word itself means "sending and taking."

Most of us meditate to bring peace and calm into our own lives. There is this concept of individualism we place on meditation that makes us think we can only help others once we've helped ourselves. The practice of Tonglen suggests that one of the best ways to find inner peace is to be kind and giving to others.

For this exercise, you will be practicing some simple elements of Tonglen through writing.

2) Pick a friend or family member you are very close to:

_____

With your eyes closed, spend a few minutes thinking about this person. Meditate on who they are, and how they're doing. In your head, start to send love their way. Energetically, provide them with anything they might need right now. Imagine yourself taking their worries and pain away. Lift the weight off their shoulders and visualize them becoming light and free.

Now let's put this to practice through writing.

Again, focus on the person you selected and meditate on who they are and how they're doing. Send love their way. Energetically provide for them with anything they may need in this moment and write it below:

»   I am sending you

»   I am sending you

»   I am sending you

»   I am sending you

»   I am sending you

»   I am sending you

Imagine yourself taking away their worries and pain:

»   I am taking away

»   I am taking away

»   I am taking away

»   I am taking away

»   I am taking away

»   I am taking away

As you lift the weight off their shoulders, send them even more love. Watch as they become light and free, and share words of kindness with them:

»   You are

»   You are

» You are

» You are

» You are

» You are

3) Now, pick someone you are in conflict with or have ill feelings toward. Perhaps this is a coworker who got the promotion you wanted or a friend who annoyed you at a party. Maybe it's someone you're jealous of whom you've never met but know of through social media.

Focus on this person and meditate on who they are and how they're doing. Send love their way. Energetically provide for them anything they may need in this moment:

» I am sending you

» I am sending you

» I am sending you

» I am sending you

» I am sending you

» I am sending you

Imagine yourself taking away their worries and pain:

» I am taking away

» I am taking away

» I am taking away

» I am taking away

» I am taking away

» I am taking away

As you lift the weight off their shoulders, send them even more love. Watch as they become light and free, and share words of kindness with them:

» You are

» You are

» You are

» You are

» You are

» You are

4) Now, think of the entire world. Feel into the Earth and its people. Think about all the nature and animals that occupy this planet. Energetically provide the world with anything it may need:

> » I am sending

> » I am sending

> » I am sending

> » I am sending

> » I am sending

> » I am sending

Imagine yourself taking away the world's worries and pain:

> » I am taking away

> » I am taking away

> » I am taking away

> » I am taking away

> » I am taking away

» I am taking away

As you free the world of all its suffering, watch as it becomes light and free. Now, share more words of kindness with it:

» You are

» You are

» You are

» You are

» You are

» You are

EXERCISE 21	DAILY CHECK-IN

As we near the end of this book, I thought it might be nice to leave you with something you can include in your daily rituals. This is a daily check-in exercise I like doing during my morning meditations. It helps set the tone for the rest of my day and is especially helpful on days my mind is racing.

If you enjoy the exercise, try adding it to your daily journaling or meditation practice. Practicing rituals can help us feel anchored.

Start the exercise by sitting in a comfortable seated position somewhere quiet. If you'd like, play some calming instrumental music. Do some stretches. Spend 5–10 minutes just being, noticing yourself, welcoming the calm if it comes, noticing the anxiety if it's there. Take deep breaths. You are imperfectly perfect, exactly how you're meant to be. Then, I want you to talk to your body and see what it says in return. Once you're finished, open your eyes and answer the following:

1) Starting at your feet and moving up to the crown of your head, what were the sensations you felt throughout the 5–10 minute meditation?

2) As you scanned your body, was there a particular area that stood out? Why do you think that is?

3) What would you like your body to know right now?

4) What does your body deserve?

5) List 15 reasons you have to be proud of yourself:

6) Any final thoughts to share with your body?

7) Repeat out loud:

I have nothing to worry about.

I can let my body relax.

Things will fall into place.

The universe is on my side.

it has been one of the greatest and most difficult years of my life. i learned everything is temporary. moments. feelings. people. flowers. i learned love is about giving. everything. and letting it hurt. i learned vulnerability is always the right choice because it is easy to be cold in a world that makes it so very difficult to remain soft. i learned all things come in twos. life and death. pain and joy. salt and sugar. me and you. it is the balance of the universe. it has been the year of hurting so bad but living so good. making friends out of strangers. making strangers out of friends. learning mint chocolate chip ice cream will fix just about everything. and for the pains it can't there will always be my mother's arms. we must learn to focus on warm energy. always. soak our limbs in it and become better lovers to the world. for if we can't learn to be kind to each other how will we ever learn to be kind to the most desperate parts of ourselves.

the sun and her flowers, page 193

CONCLUSION

LOVE LETTER TO THE WRITER/READER

The idea for this book came to me while facilitating writing workshops on Instagram Live during the COVID-19 pandemic. It was such an anxious and uncertain time, and I longed to connect with other people because, at the end of the day, each other is all we have.

Facilitating those workshops showed me how many of us needed permission to take 10 minutes out of our day to write for ourselves. As I facilitated these workshops and invited my readers to share their work, I was blown away by their creativity. There wasn't a single person whose words didn't leave me speechless. It was incredible to witness what they could create during a 10-minute writing exercise.

Through these exercises, I hope you learned something about yourself and got a sense of the power you possess. I hope this book gave you the space to reflect, process, and grow.

Our voices are so powerful. I hope you feel the strength of yours.

WHAT'S NEXT?

The journey isn't over—it's just beginning.

You now have an entire book of words you've written. If you would like to do more with these pieces, transfer them to a journal or computer to edit and revise. You could take anything you've written here and turn it into a poem, play, song, or short story.

If you'd like to make writing a more sustainable part of your life, repeat these exercises in a separate journal. You'll be amazed at how the same prompts pull something different out of you each time. Feel free to alter these exercises in any way you like or use them as inspiration to develop your own.

Most of all, remember that you don't need me or these exercises to help you write. You are creative by nature. Nothing can ever change that.

Sending you infinite love,

Rupi

ABOUT THE AUTHOR

RUPI KAUR is a poet, artist, and performer. As a 21-year-old university student Rupi wrote, illustrated, and self-published her first poetry collection, *milk and honey*. Next came its artistic sibling, *the sun and her flowers*. These collections have sold over 10 million copies and have been translated into over 40 languages. Her latest collection, *home body*, debuted #1 on bestseller lists across the world. As she has done in all things from the very beginning, Rupi self-produced *Rupi Kaur Live*, the first poetry special of its kind, which debuted on Amazon Prime Video in 2021. Rupi's work touches on love, loss, trauma, healing, femininity, and migration. She feels most at home when creating art, performing her poetry onstage, and spending time with family and friends.

ACKNOWLEDGMENTS

I would like to give a special thank-you to the incredible people who made this book possible.

Thank you, Rakhi Mutta, for inspiring me to take the idea for this book and run with it. You are the greatest friend, guardian, manager, and partner in business anyone could ask for.

Thank you, Rattanamol Singh, for your commitment to excellence. Your genius allows the rest of us to feign a bit of brilliance every now and then. Thank you for your endless dedication to everything I create and share.

Thank you to my mighty team for helping me level up with each edit. Mahsa Sajadi, Ashleigh Collins, Prabh Saini, Baljit Singh, and Jessica Huang, thank you for going through each exercise and providing critical feedback. I can't imagine what this book would've looked like if you hadn't been a part of it. Shannon Frost and Angella Fajardo, your eagle eyes caught things the rest of us didn't. Thanks for being involved in the editing, which can sometimes be a tedious and laborious part of book writing. You never showed signs of slowing down. I am so grateful to do this work with a team of amazing young women.

Thank you to my publisher, Andrews McMeel Publishing, for making this book come to life with passion and dedication. Kirsty Melville, thank you for always fighting for me. You champion my words and vision like no other. Patty Rice, thank you for being my editor on this book, and every other. Julie Barnes, thank you for bringing my visual design dreams to life. It's been so fun and such an honor to create beautiful books with you. What a team we are.

Andrews McMeel Publishing
a division of Andrews McMeel Universal
1130 Walnut Street, Kansas City, Missouri 64106

www.andrewsmcmeel.com

All references to published poems refer to the paperback editions.

22 23 24 25 26 POA 10 9 8 7 6 5 4 3 2

ISBN: 978-1-5248-7326-4

Library of Congress Control Number: 2021942999

Illustrations and cover design by Rupi Kaur

ATTENTION: SCHOOLS AND BUSINESSES
Andrews McMeel books are available at quantity discounts with
bulk purchase for educational, business, or sales promotional use.
For information, please e-mail the Andrews McMeel Publishing
Special Sales Department: specialsales@amuniversal.com.